A LOOK AT WEATHER

MONSOONS

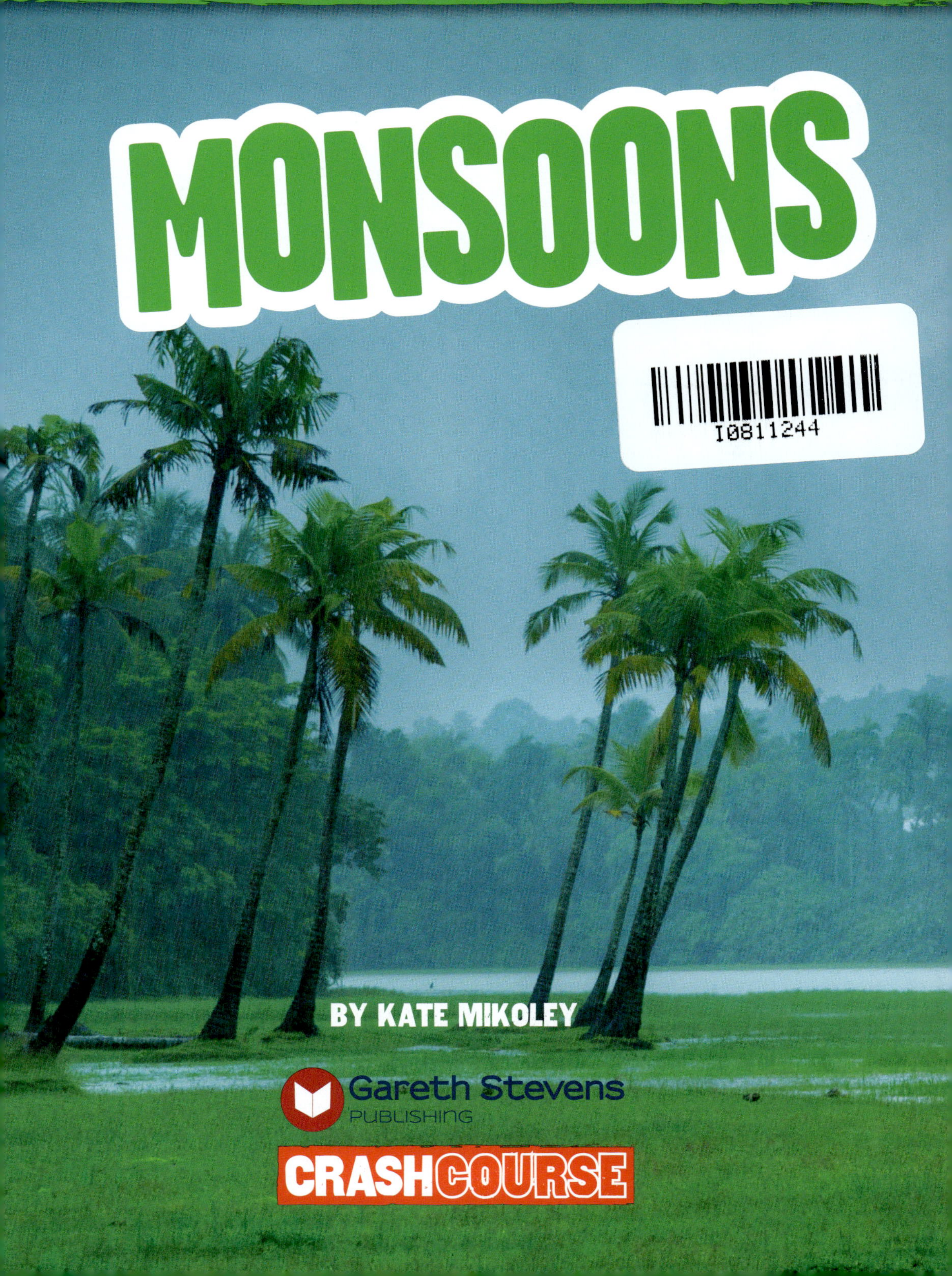

BY KATE MIKOLEY

Gareth Stevens PUBLISHING

CRASHCOURSE

Please visit our website, www.garethstevens.com. For a free color catalog of all our high-quality books, call toll free 1-800-542-2595 or fax 1-877-542-2596.

Library of Congress Cataloging-in-Publication Data

Names: Mikoley, Kate.
Title: Monsoons/ Kate Mikoley.
Description: New York : Gareth Stevens Publishing, 2024. | Series: A look at weather| Includes glossary, index, and bibliographic information
Identifiers: ISBN 9781538287316 (pbk) | ISBN 9781538287323 (library bound) | ISBN 9781538287330 (ebook)
Subjects: LCSH: Monsoons-- Juvenile literature
Classification: LCC QC939.M7 M55 2024 | DDC 551. 55--dc24

First Edition

Published in 2024 by
Gareth Stevens Publishing
2544 Clinton Street
Buffalo, NY 14224

Designer: Karen Quigley
Editor: Kate Mikoley

Photo credits: Cover, p. 1 Milju varghese/Shutterstock.com; pp. 2-3 kzww/Shutterstock.com; wind symbol JuliMur/Shutterstock.com; warm/cold front symbols NickJulia/Shutterstock.com; series art (cloud background) ekapol sirachainan/Shutterstock.com; series art (cartoon cloud) MimaCZ/Shutterstock.com; p. 5 Bardocz Peter/Shutterstock.com; p. 7 nektofadeev/Shutterstock.com; p. 9 Hafidz Abdul Kadir/Shutterstock.com; p. 11 Tonio_75/Shutterstock.com; p. 13 cookelma/iStock.com; p. 15 pixelfusion3d/iStock.com; p. 17 f9photos /iStock.com; p. 19 File:The Himalayas (48625198948)/commons.wikimedia.org; p. 21 Gam1983/iStock.com; p. 23 Balaji Srinivasan/iStock.com; p. 23 (sign) Cherrapunji/commons.wikimedia.org; p. 25 Mike Hardiman/Shutterstock.com; p. 27 Manoej Paateel/Shutterstock.com; p. 29 File: India monsoon imerg 13-20 august 2018/commons.wikimedia.org; p. 30 courtesy of the NOAA.

Printed in the United States of America

CPSIA compliance information: Batch #CS24GS: For further information contact Gareth Stevens at 1-800-542-2595.

CONTENTS

Words in the glossary appear in **bold** type the first time they are used in the text.

WHAT'S A MONSOON?

When you hear about a monsoon, you might think of lots of heavy rain. However, a monsoon is actually a kind of wind system. Monsoons can cause rain and wet seasons, but they also cause dry seasons.

Make the Grade

Monsoons happen in much of the **tropics**, like South Asia, including in India, Sri Lanka, and Bangladesh.

A monsoon is a change in the wind direction in a certain **region** based on the time of year. These winds change directions between winter and summer. Monsoons make for wet summers and dry winters.

Make the Grade

The monsoons that cause the most rainfall happen near the Indian Ocean.

SUMMER MONSOONS

As seasons change, the **temperature** of land and the water nearby are different. For example, in summer, the land in a monsoon region is hot. So is the air above the land. However, the sea nearby and the air above it are colder.

Make the Grade

Monsoons blow from cold areas to warmer areas.

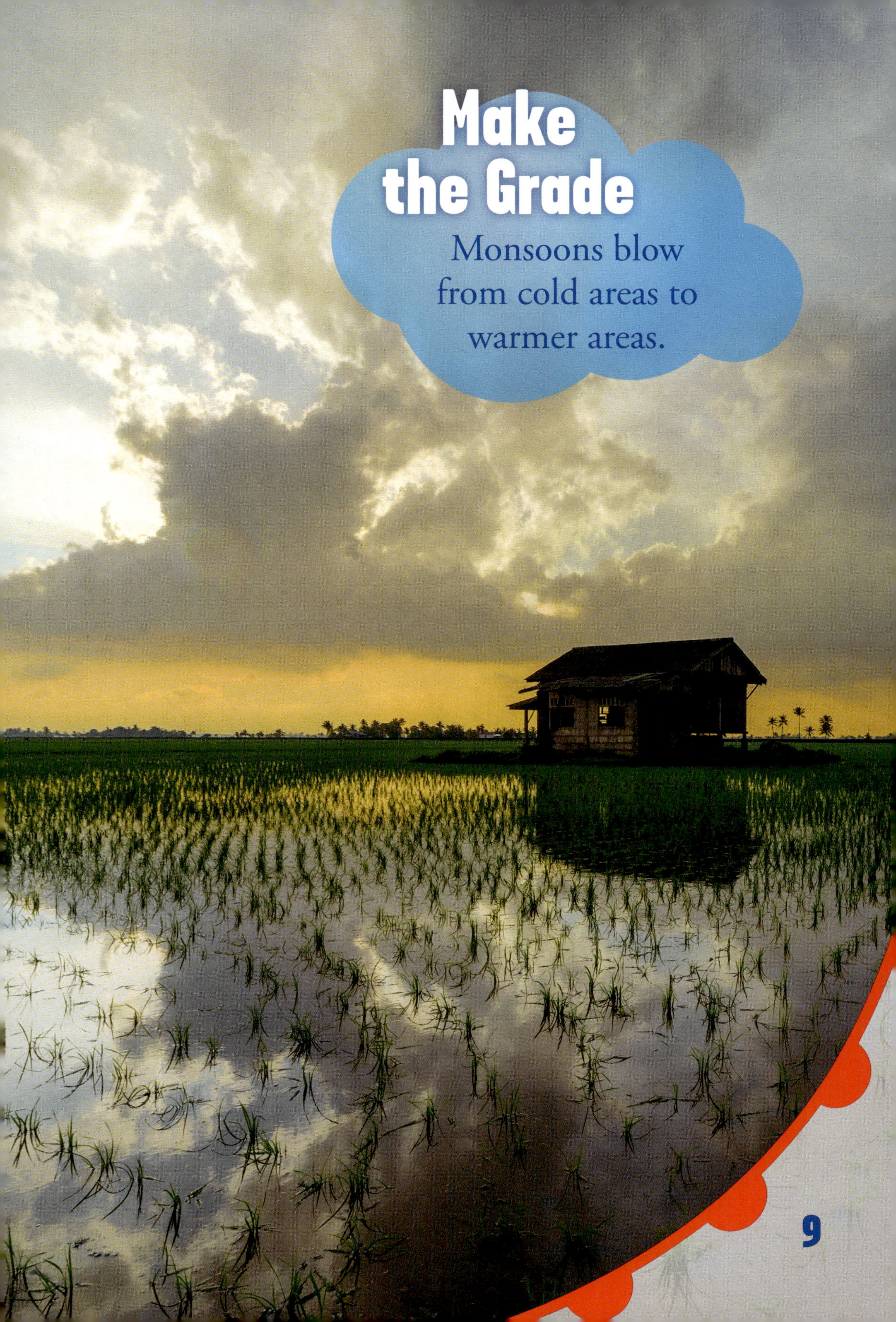

Hot air is lighter than cold air. That's why hot air rises. During a summer monsoon, the colder air above the sea blows in to take the place of the hot air above land.

Make the Grade

Summer monsoon winds carry **moisture** that has **evaporated** from sea water. This moisture meets the warm air over land and falls as heavy rain.

WINTER MONSOONS

In a winter monsoon, the air above land is colder than the air above the sea. Since it's warmer, the sea air rises. The colder land air blows out to sea to take the place of the ocean air. This makes for a dry winter on land.

Make the Grade

Most of the time, winter monsoons come from the east and summer monsoons come from the west.

EFFECTS OF MONSOONS

Countries with summer monsoons see lots of effects, such as **humidity** and rain. Flooding and **mudslides** are just some of the dangers that come along with these monsoons. In some cities, it's normal for streets to flood 1.5 feet (0.5 m) every summer!

Make the Grade

Mudslides can cover farmland with water and mud, and ruin crops.

While summer monsoons are often dangerous, some places need them. In India and Southeast Asia, the heavy rain is important for growing crops such as rice and tea. The rain also supplies water to be used the rest of the year.

Make the Grade

Monsoon rains help grass grow, keeping cows on dairy farms in India healthy and fed.

When people think of monsoons, they often think of the wet summer monsoons. This is likely because winter monsoons have fewer effects. In South and Southeast Asia, winter monsoons are much less powerful because the Himalaya mountains block the wind and rain.

Make the Grade

One dangerous weather event that can be caused by winter monsoons is a drought. This is a time of very little **precipitation**. This can harm crops and lead to food and water **shortages**.

MONSOONS AND ELECTRICITY

Places that get monsoons often use **hydroelectric** power. The water gathered during the monsoons can power whole communities. If a monsoon doesn't drop enough rain, this kind of electricity, or power, can go into short supply—and become costly!

Make the Grade

Electricity is needed for hospitals, schools, and other important businesses. When it's in short supply, only those who can pay a lot of money may be able to use it.

MAJOR MONSOONS

In South Asia's summer monsoon, commonly known as the Indian monsoon, the wind blows from the Indian Ocean to India. Some of the rainiest places in the world get most of their rain as a result of the Indian monsoon.

Make the Grade

Cherrapunjee, a town in northeastern India, commonly gets more than 107 inches (273 cm) of rain in just the month of July!

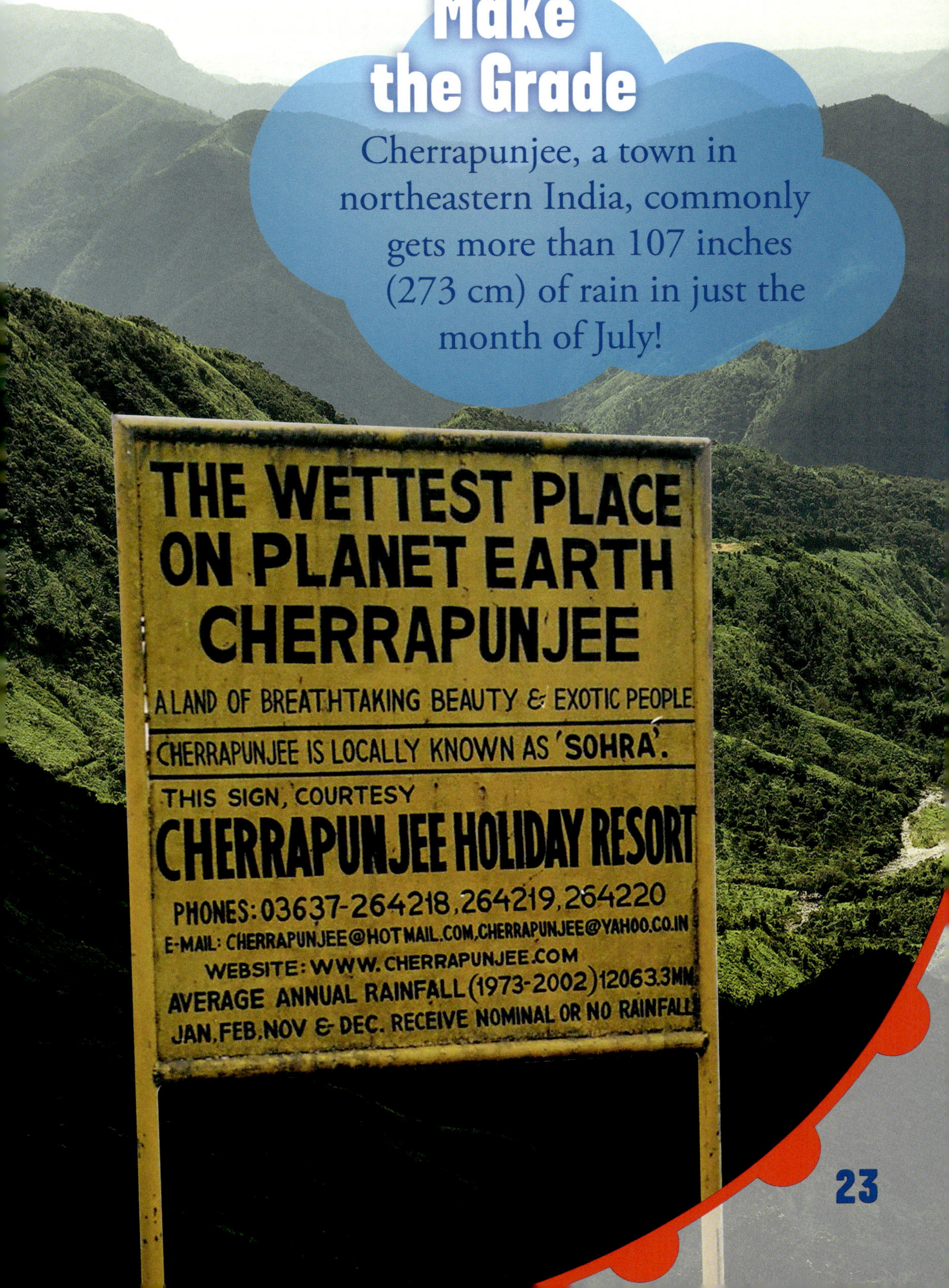

Beyond South Asia, monsoons also happen in West Africa, Australia, and parts of Central America. The North American monsoon happens when winds blow north off the Pacific Ocean during summer and south from the land during winter.

Make the Grade

The North American monsoon can help fight wildfires in hot and dry areas of the Southwestern United States.

A PERFECT BALANCE

Monsoons can be heavier or lighter from year to year. Too little rain can mean crops fail, leaving people hungry and farmers with little money. Too much rain, however, can cause flooding. This can also ruin crops and drown **livestock**.

Make the Grade

The timing of a monsoon matters too. If the summer monsoon is later than usual, there may be food and electricity shortages.

For a monsoon to be helpful, it must come at just the right time and bring just enough rain—but not too much! This is tricky. If you live in a place with monsoons, you must always be prepared.

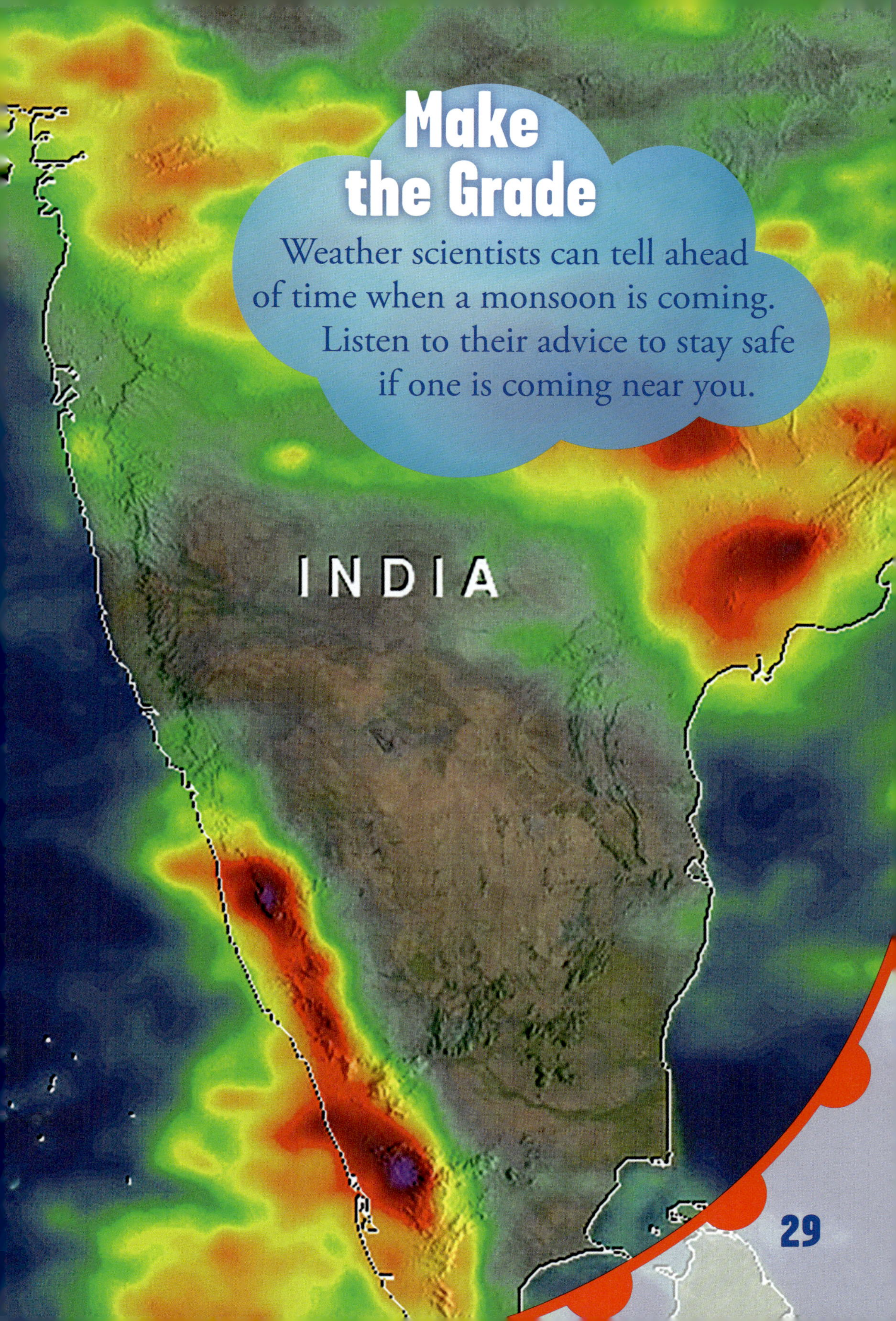

Make the Grade

Weather scientists can tell ahead of time when a monsoon is coming. Listen to their advice to stay safe if one is coming near you.

MAKING A MONSOON

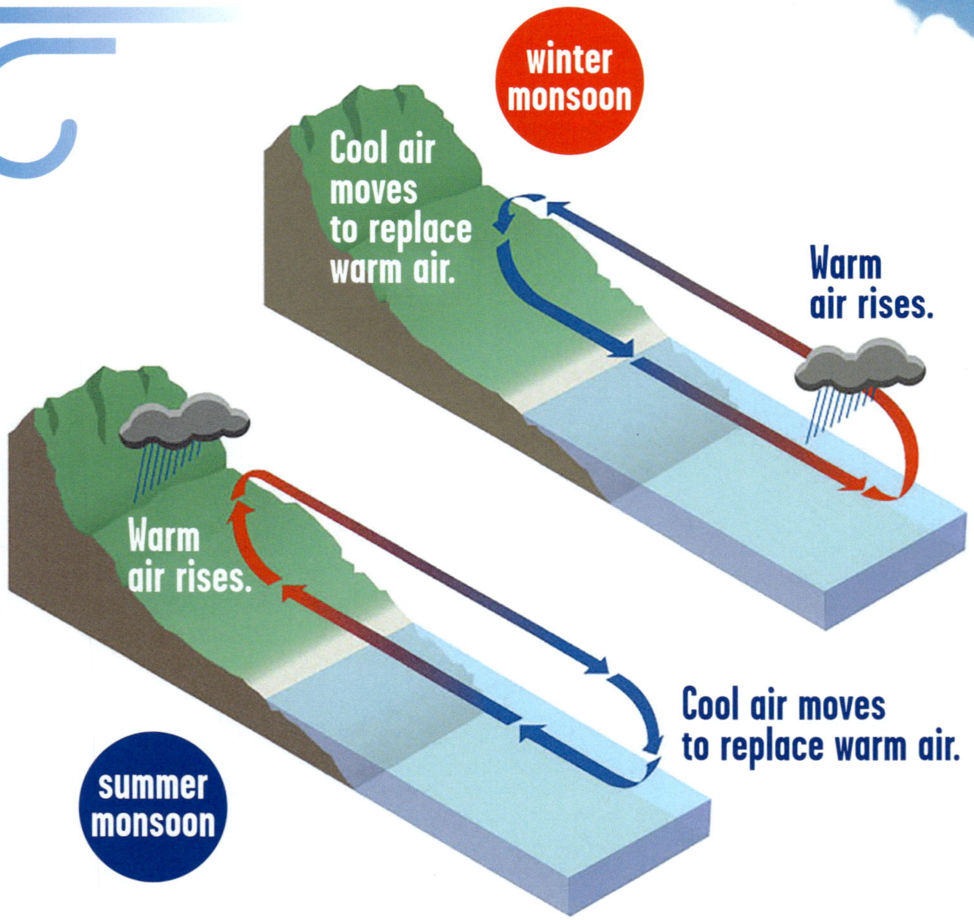

GLOSSARY

evaporate: To change from a liquid to a gas.

humidity: Moisture in the air.

hydroelectric: Having to do with creating power using the movement of water.

livestock: Animals kept or raised, often on a farm.

precipitation: Rain, snow, sleet, or hail.

moisture: Water in the air.

mudslide: A moving mass of mud made up of soil and rainwater or melted snow.

region: A large area of land that has features that make it different from nearby areas of land.

shortage: A lack of something.

temperature: How hot or cold something is.

tropics: The areas of Earth surrounding the equator.

FOR MORE INFORMATION

BOOKS

Farndon, John, Sean Callery, and Miranda Smith. *Weather*. New York, NY: Scholastic, 2020.

Winch, Anne. *Floods: Causes and Effects.* Mankato, MN: 12-Story Library, 2022.

WEBSITE

Monsoon
education.nationalgeographic.org/resource/monsoon
This page has even more facts about monsoons.

Publisher's note to educators and parents: Our editors have carefully reviewed these websites to ensure that they are suitable for students. Many websites change frequently, however, and we cannot guarantee that a site's future contents will continue to meet our high standards of quality and educational value. Be advised that students should be closely supervised whenever they access the internet.

INDEX